MW00963688

By Divine Stationaries

Name

Advice / Thoughts / Wishes

Name

Advice / Thoughts / Wishes

Name   Advice / Thoughts / Wishes

------------------------------------   --

------------------------------------   --

------------------------------------   --

------------------------------------   --

Name

Advice / Thoughts / Wishes

--   --

--   --

--   --

--   --

Names

Advice / Thoughts / Messages

Names   Advice / Thoughts / Wishes

--   --

--   --

--   --

--   --

Names   Advice / Thoughts / Wishes

-------------------------------------   ---

-------------------------------------   ---

-------------------------------------   ---

-------------------------------------   ---

Names   Advice / Thoughts / Wishes

--   --

--   --

--   --

--   --

Names   Advice / Thoughts / Wishes

------------------------------------   --

------------------------------------   --

------------------------------------   --

------------------------------------   --

Names

Advice / Thoughts / Wishes

Names   Advice / Thoughts / Wishes

------------------------------------   --

------------------------------------   --

------------------------------------   --

------------------------------------   --

Names

Advice / Thoughts / Wishes

Names

Advice / Thoughts / Wishes

Names   Advice / Thoughts / Wishes

--   --

--   --

--   --

--   --

Names   Advice / Thoughts / Wishes

--   ---

--   ---

--   ---

--   ---

Names

Advice / Thoughts / Wishes

Names

Advice / Thoughts / Wishes

Names   Advice / Thoughts / Wishes

-------------------------------------   ---

-------------------------------------   ---

-------------------------------------   ---

-------------------------------------   ---

Names

Advice / Thoughts / Wishes

Names   Advice / Thoughts / Wishes

--   ---

--   ---

--   ---

--   ---

Names

Advice / Thoughts / Wishes

Names   Advice / Thoughts / Wishes

------------------------------------   --

------------------------------------   --

------------------------------------   --

------------------------------------   --

Names

Advice / Thoughts / Wishes

Names

Advice / Thoughts / Wishes

Names

Advice / Thoughts / Wishes

Names

Advice / Thoughts / Wishes

Names

Advice / Thoughts / Wishes

Names   Advice / Thoughts / Wishes

---   --

---   --

---   --

---   --

Names

Advice / Thoughts / Wishes

Names   Advice / Thoughts / Wishes

--   --

--   --

--   --

--   --

Names   Advice / Thoughts / Wishes

-------------------------------------   --

-------------------------------------   --

-------------------------------------   --

-------------------------------------   --

Names

Advice / Thoughts / Wishes

Names

Advice / Thoughts / Wishes

Names

Advice / Thoughts / Wishes

Names

Advice / Thoughts / Wishes

Names

Advice / Thoughts / Wishes

-- --

-- --

-- --

-- --

Names

Advice / Thoughts / Wishes

Names

Advice / Thoughts / Wishes

Names

Advice / Thoughts / Wishes

Names   Advice / Thoughts / Wishes

--   ---

--   ---

--   ---

--   ---

Names   Advice / Thoughts / Wishes

------------------------------------   --

------------------------------------   --

------------------------------------   --

------------------------------------   --

Names   Advice / Thoughts / Wishes

--   ---

--   ---

--   ---

--   ---

Names

Advice / Thoughts / Wishes

Names   Advice / Thoughts / Wishes

--   --

--   --

--   --

--   --

Names

Advice / Thoughts / Wishes

Names   Advice / Thoughts / Wishes

--   --

--   --

--   --

--   --

Names   Advice / Thoughts / Wishes

--   --

--   --

--   --

--   --

Names   Advice / Thoughts / Wishes

-------------------------------------   --

-------------------------------------   --

-------------------------------------   --

-------------------------------------   --

Names

Advice / Thoughts / Wishes

Names   Advice / Thoughts / Wishes

---------------------------------------   --

---------------------------------------   --

---------------------------------------   --

---------------------------------------   --

Names

Advice / Thoughts / Wishes

Names   Advice / Thoughts / Wishes

--   --

--   --

--   --

--   --

Names

Advice / Thoughts / Wishes

Names   Advice / Thoughts / Wishes

--   ---

--   ---

--   ---

--   ---

Names

Advice / Thoughts / Wishes

Names   Advice / Thoughts / Wishes

------------------------------------   --

------------------------------------   --

------------------------------------   --

------------------------------------   --

Names

Advice / Thoughts / Wishes

Names

Advice / Thoughts / Wishes

Names

Advice / Thoughts / Wishes

Names

Advice / Thoughts / Wishes

Names

Advice / Thoughts / Wishes

Names   Advice / Thoughts / Wishes

--   ---

--   ---

--   ---

--   ---

Names

Advice / Thoughts / Wishes

Names   Advice / Thoughts / Wishes

--   --

--   --

--   --

--   --

Names

Advice / Thoughts / Wishes

Names

Advice / Thoughts / Wishes

Names

Advice / Thoughts / Wishes

Names

Advice / Thoughts / Wishes

Names

Advice / Thoughts / Wishes

Names   Advice / Thoughts / Wishes

--   ---

--   ---

--   ---

--   ---

Names

Advice / Thoughts / Wishes

Names

Advice / Thoughts / Wishes

Names

Advice / Thoughts / Wishes

Names

Advice / Thoughts / Wishes

Names

Advice / Thoughts / Wishes

Names

Advice / Thoughts / Wishes

Names

Advice / Thoughts / Wishes

Names

Advice / Thoughts / Wishes

--   --

--   --

--   --

--   --

Names

Advice / Thoughts / Wishes

Names

Advice / Thoughts / Wishes

Names

Advice / Thoughts / Wishes

Names

Advice / Thoughts / Wishes

Names

Advice / Thoughts / Wishes

Names

Advice / Thoughts / Wishes

Names   Advice / Thoughts / Wishes

--   --

--   --

--   --

--   --

Add Photo

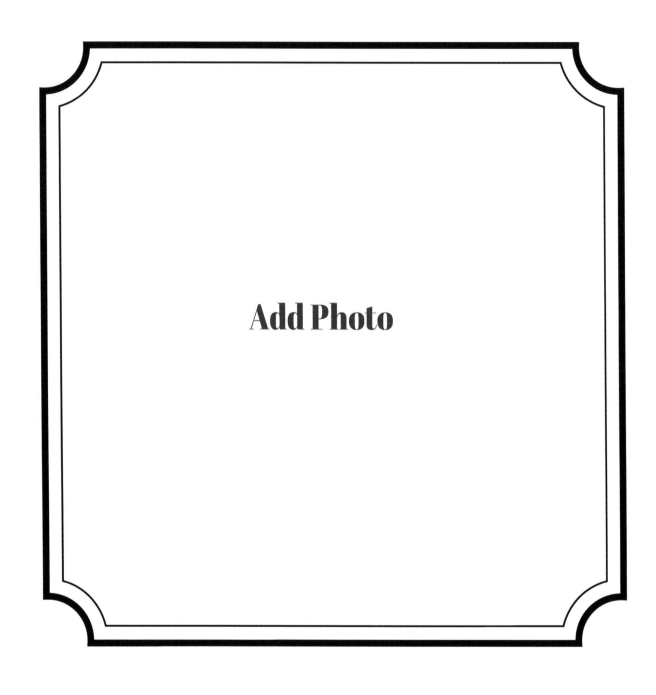

Add Photo

Add Photo

Add Photo

Add Photo

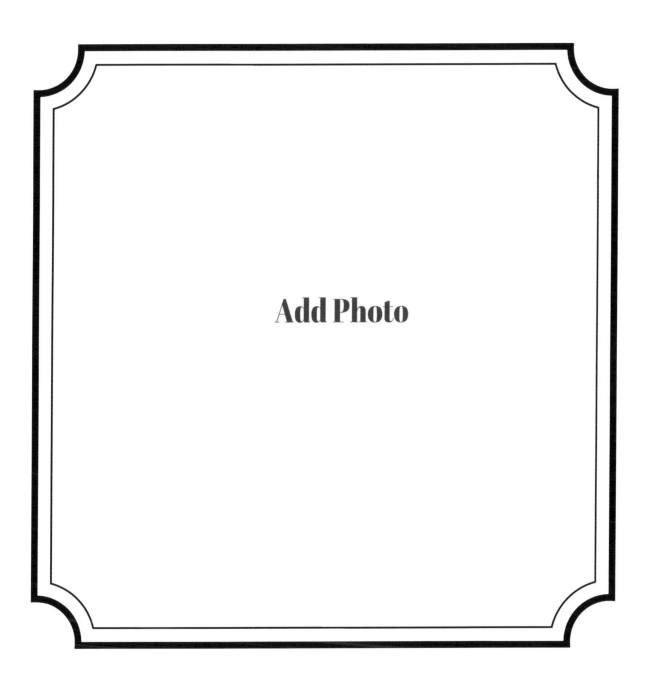

Add Photo

Add Photo

Gift Log

DATE	GIFT DESCRIPTION	GIVEN BY	THANK YOU NOTICE SENT

Gift Log

DATE	GIFT DESCRIPTION	GIVEN BY	THANK YOU NOTICE SENT

Gift Log

DATE	GIFT DESCRIPTION	GIVEN BY	THANK YOU NOTICE SENT

Gift Log

DATE	GIFT DESCRIPTION	GIVEN BY	THANK YOU NOTICE SENT

Gift Log

DATE	GIFT DESCRIPTION	GIVEN BY	THANK YOU NOTICE SENT

Gift Log

DATE	GIFT DESCRIPTION	GIVEN BY	THANK YOU NOTICE SENT

Manufactured by Amazon.ca
Bolton, ON